DAVE MORTON lived in Wibsey, Bradford, in the (then) West Riding of Yorkshire until the age of twelve.

His father was a noted Bradford League cricketer, and early memories are of watching Harry Morton bat for Great Horton Cricket Club, and seeing the fine Yorkshire County Cricket Club team of those days strutting their stuff at Park Avenue, just down the road.

Late in 1955 the family moved to the Midlands. After completing his formal education at Cambridge University, in 1966 Dave was finally free to move back up north, to a job in Manchester, where he has lived ever since.

For the next thirty-six years, he played league cricket in the Manchester area, for Prestwich CC and Newton Heath CC.

Following early retirement (from work, not from cricket), Dave joined Yorkshire CCC as a member in time for the 1994 season. He continued to turn out for his club second team until he was sixty, apart from missing a season to have a hip replaced.

Dave is now one of the many travelling supporters who follow Yorkshire round the country. He has always watched

a few Lancashire games
member of the Red Rose
England tour, but it is fo
the greatest pleasure.

SWEET SHIRES

Dave Morton

Published in 2016 by SilverWood Books

SilverWood Books Ltd
14 Small Street, Bristol, BS1 1DE, United Kingdom
www.silverwoodbooks.co.uk

ISBN 978-1-78132-526-1

British Library Cataloguing in Publication Data
A CIP catalogue record for this book is available from the British Library

Printed in the UK by Latimer Trend & Company Ltd
on responsibly sourced paper

CONTENTS

The Proud Cricketer 6
Introduction 7
1 Derbyshire 9
2 Staffordshire 13
3 Manchester 15
Photo section 1 17
4 Durham 35
5 Glamorgan 37
6 Kent 39
7 Leicestershire 42
8 Sussex 44
9 Essex 46
10 Middlesex 47
11 Nottinghamshire 48
Photo Section 2 49
12 Lancashire 65
13 Northamptonshire 68
14 Worcestershire 70
15 Hampshire 72
16 Gloucestershire 74
17 Somerset 76
18 Warwickshire 78
19 Surrey 80
Photo Section 3 81
20 Yorkshire 95
21 Scarborough 100
A Note on the Photography 103
List of Photographs 106

THE PROUD CRICKETER

England hath played at many a game, and ever her toy was a ball;
But the meadow game, with the beautiful name, is king and lord of them all,
Cricket is king and lord of them all, through the sweet green English shires;
And here's to the bat, and the ball (How's that?), and the heart that never tires.

O, the glance of the bat, and the dip of the ball, as it hums through
 the crouching slips,
O, the buzzing wail of the flying bail, and the grin on the bowler's lips;
O, the blind, blind swipe, and the cut that's caught, and the terribly quick throw in;
Ah, here's to the wit of the bat (Well hit!), and here's to the ball with a spin.

The soul is glad in the thick o' the game, a song through the spirit swims,
For the brain is king of the muscles' swing and lord of the eager limbs;
And it's joy, pure joy, for the hearts of men, the clean, the strong, and the sage,
Till the pulse is cold, and we're out (Well bowled!) to a flattering lob from Age.

O, it's sweet to talk through the summer eves of the games we have lost and won,
Of the quick-turned wrist, of the shooting twist, of the catch and the stolen run;
It's good to show on the stinging hand how the hot return was stopped;
And what of my duck, if we lost? (Hard luck!) – but what of the catch you dropped?

But when we are puffing through middle life, and it's time for the last sweet
 knocks,
When our average falls, and we fear fast balls, and the young 'uns call us crocks;
Well, watching the young 'uns play will serve, and still with our latest breath –
"Well played!" we'll shout from the ropes (Not out!) – and follow the game till
 death.

Harold Begbie

INTRODUCTION

You skipped Begbie's poem. Of course you did. You've probably skipped this introduction, too; but now you're enjoying the photos and, perhaps, some of my anecdotes. You will eventually return here.

Now read the poem.

It was written over a hundred years ago. The 'quick-turned wrist' and the 'shooting twist' sound a bit dated, it's true, a bit obscure; and the 'meadow game, with the beautiful name' suggests Begbie might be one of those people (southerners, usually) who think cricket beautiful without understanding that what it really is, is battle. Combat. Warfare.

Beauty is not the purpose of the game; it is a by-product of excellence.

However, Begbie does understand battle, and sadness, too. He knows about 'puffing through middle life', the fear of facing a fast bowler when you're old and slow on your feet. He has experienced the post-match recriminations after his team has lost, and received the big send-off from the bowler who has made his bails fly; perhaps only a grin, back in 1905.

I am glad I discovered these verses while I was still playing. Every April, fielding with the trees bare but the air sweet, I would recall verse three. How joyful it was to be alive and playing cricket in another green English spring, with all of summer still stretching ahead.

I was old enough by then to know it wouldn't last for ever, but Begbie has touched on just about everything I love about cricket, all in those few brief verses.

Now, many years later, I am happy to follow cricket – mostly Yorkshire CCC – round the sweet shires of England

and Wales; never forget Wales. Photography is my old man's hobby, and if I am able to combine my two passions into one enjoyable little book, if I can share just a little of my pleasure, I will be content enough.

My journey begins in Derbyshire and Staffordshire, where my own adult playing life began. Then it's on to Manchester and the rest of the country, with no more order or rhyme and reason than an ECB fixture list.

Enjoy the photos; and forgive me, you good people of Kent. I love you really.

Dave, May 2016

1

DERBYSHIRE – CRICKET'S BEST-KEPT SECRET

So where is the prettiest First Class ground in all of England? Worcester? Gorgeous. Arundel? A bit twee, but nice. Taunton? Yes, good call. Tunbridge Wells? You've got to be joking! You need to get out more.

Actually, the answer is…Chesterfield. By a mile.

It's also a damn good cricket ground, with a pitch that rewards the best players, batsmen and bowlers alike.

My memories of Chesterfield? Back when I was a kid, the awesome, terrible Jackson and his mate Gladwin, battering batsmen black and blue. I probably read about it more than actually observed it, to be honest. I was definitely there in July 1994 when Warwickshire, with Lara, faced Devon Malcolm and Dominic Cork. It was one of the most spectacular days of cricket I have ever seen, 445 runs and sixteen wickets, all on the first day of a championship match.

Brian Lara made 142.

Another little memory, early season this time, freezing, too cold for anywhere to be beautiful. I was standing on the pathway, square on the off side, just over the boundary boards. I was dressed as I would be for a winter rugby match: heavy overcoat, cup of hot coffee in my right hand.

Devon Malcolm, fast and short and wide; Richard Blakey, trademark square cut, one-bounce four, travelling fast. I stuck out my left hand and caught it, clean as a whistle. A little knot of Derbyshire supporters five yards away applauded me for not spilling my coffee; and then they laughed at my girlie attempted left-handed throw-in.

My pictures of Chesterfield, however, were taken on a glorious day in July 2013.

This was the game in which a young Yorkshire opening

batsman made just 275 not out. Well batted, Alex Lees! The sun shone, the birds sang and God was in his Yorkshire heaven. There was a packed crowd to enjoy it, too.

If Chesterfield is Derbyshire's jewel, let's not forget other grounds. For a few years, in my teens and early twenties, I lived in Burton-on-Trent. Our house was on the Staffordshire side of the river, as indeed was the Ind Coope Brewery ground where Derbyshire used to play one game per season; just an easy downhill cycle ride from where I lived.

I experienced my first adult cricket in Burton, turning out for the Marston's Brewery team, so I played several away games at the bigger, grander Ind Coope ground. Once, I disgraced myself.

It was all proper cricket in those days, none of this limited overs stuff, and I was batting as Marston's were trying to hold on for a draw. I was facing the Ind Coope pro, a guy called Mick Groves, a leg-spinner who had some First Class experience with Warwickshire, I believe.

I was playing him mostly with my pad, as you could in those days, as long as you got outside the line. This particular ball hit me full-toss on the boot, way outside the off-stump. It was not out under the Laws of the time. It would be not out today, too, but he screamed at the umpire, "That was my googly! My googly!" The man was their umpire and he gave me out. I rather cracked a bit, though I said only one word.

We'd call the event 'bollocks-gate', these days. My father was not amused. You should NOT swear at umpires. Ever. He was right. But umpires shouldn't bloody cheat, should they? And a pro should be ashamed of himself for getting out a young kid in that fashion.

The First Class game I particularly remember at that venue was played in August 1958, when I would have been fourteen, a couple of years earlier than the above 'incident'.

Hampshire were the visitors, with Colin Ingleby-Mackenzie, to name just several of them, and it rained most of the first day. Just a few minutes' play were possible, in which time Derbyshire made 8 for one.

The second day was 'interesting'. Derbyshire were all out for 74, Hampshire replied with 23 (that man Jackson, again!), Derbyshire made 107 and Hampshire improved to make 55 in their second innings.

Thirty-nine wickets had fallen in the day. Real cricket!

By covering pitches we have deprived ourselves – and the bowlers – of a lot of fun.

The loss of 'outgrounds' like Ind Coope is also to be regretted. Of the County Ground at Derby I have few memories. It is a much more pleasant place nowadays than it was back then, but I have no photo of the necessary quality.

The only memory of my last visit to Derby is of a shirtless, middle-aged spectator. It was freezing. "Oh, he never wears a shirt," said a guy sitting nearby. Of the cricket that day, I can recall nothing.

I have two more Derbyshire grounds for your enjoyment. There's Glossop, where I played many times. Once, by now an experienced player, I batted throughout an entire 50-over innings for fourteen not out, and a vital league point for a losing-draw. That was fun, though eleven Glossop lads would not agree.

Glossop is a lovely place to play cricket, and to watch, if you get a nice summer's day. The drawback is you don't see many of those up in the Derbyshire hills, but my photo was taken on one such, when Derbyshire 2nd XI v Lancashire was the match, in May 2004.

The Author batting at Glossop in 1984

John Simpson, the current Middlesex wicketkeeper and then a very young boy of fifteen, was in the Lancs XI.

My final Derbyshire photo comes from the gorgeous Belper Meadows CC, where Derbys 2s were playing their Yorkshire counterparts. Joe Sayers got a hundred for the White Rose that green April day in 2011.

Sadly, I have no photograph of the Ind Coope ground in Burton, but Derbyshire is a lovely county and a lovely place to watch cricket. If you have never been to Queen's Park, Chesterfield, that is an omission you need to correct, before the venue disappears from our ever-dwindling First Class list.

2

STAFFORDSHIRE BEGINNINGS

It is a historical anomaly that thinly populated Derbyshire should become the First Class County, and that Staffordshire had to submit to the role of Minor County.

I left Yorkshire as an already cricket-obsessed twelve-year-old and, as I have remarked, I lived in Burton-on-Trent, Staffordshire, through my teenage years. For four years I attended Denstone College in that same county, and at eighteen I spent the summer of 1962 as a sandwich course student at the huge English Electric Company in Stafford itself.

It was here I experienced my first taste of league cricket. Only minor stuff, on some pretty rough pitches, but I enjoyed it at the time. I seem to remember that out of the twenty-two players on the two English Electric teams, ten of us were from Yorkshire.

I played in one match in which we batted first and, from the depths of 25 for nine, we won by 65 runs!

The heroes were our two opening bowlers, batsmen ten and eleven – one a big lump of a Yorkshireman, the other, slim and lithe, from the Caribbean. They slogged 75 for the last wicket before combining to skittle out the opposition for 35.

In another game, the contest went right to the wire, the very last ball. It was dark, the opposition needed five to win and nine wickets were down. Their number eleven was reputed to be blind in one eye, and our big Yorkshire quickie was bowling to him.

I can't remember his name after all these years, but our man had a slower delivery of which he was immensely proud. He decided this was the time to bowl it.

I can still picture the ball disappearing out of the ground, briefly illuminated by the bright lights in the street, before passing into eternal darkness. "Ridiculous ball," said our captain, who was a bit of a toff, with a posh accent.

"If you don't like the [bleep] way I bowl don't [bleep] pick me," was the response. And that was that. End of, as they say these days.

So I moved on, to Cambridge University, then to a job in Manchester, where I played all my real cricket.

For my Staffordshire picture I have chosen Stone CC, where Lancashire played the Minor County in the first round of the Cheltenham & Gloucester Trophy in 2004. Pretty surroundings, though I never had the privilege of playing there myself.

It is to be regretted that club cricketers are now denied these games against the top professionals, and that clubs like Stone are not able to enjoy their big day in the sun. The game of cricket is the poorer.

3

CLUB CRICKET IN MANCHESTER

In 1966 I came to Manchester and I have lived here ever since. It's not too bad in Prestwich, only forty minutes from Headingley if the M62 is flowing, and two hours from Scarborough.

It was playing in Manchester that shaped me as a cricketer. Understanding that, at twenty-three, I was not much of a player at all was the vital first step in the learning process. At Prestwich CC, under the guidance of Ken Morgan, a fine player and a great man, I soon became a solid 1st XI player at the decent (but far from elite) level that was the Lancashire & Cheshire League.

I had been nowhere near getting on my school 1st XI, so for me to play at that level was an achievement. I thought so, anyway.

We enjoyed our cricket, without ever actually threatening to win anything. Later, we developed a slightly more abrasive edge to our game, but the league as a whole was quite laid-back and friendly – with exceptions, as always.

My photo of Prestwich CC is a recent one, from 2015. The current team is a level above ours of the 1970s, and so are the facilities: clubhouse, dressing rooms and pitch. It is wonderful to see the club thriving, including a strong Junior Section. Middle-class clubs like Prestwich are doing okay; it's the inner city that is the worry.

Back in the late '60s, the L&C League's star player was Frank Hayes of Marple CC. He went on to play for Lancashire and England.

There were others, notably Norman McVicker of Stand CC, who became a key member of Ray Illingworth's championship-winning Leicestershire side. Tony Durose, of Dukinfield CC, played for Northamptonshire. Glossop's David Wilde played a few games for Derbyshire. A left-arm bowler, he was a big, rough handful for the amateur batsman to face. Great fun!

Over the years that followed, the L&C League nurtured two more Test players, Mike Atherton of Woodhouses CC and Warren Hegg who, like McVicker, was from Stand. I was the same age as Durose and the club-cricketer fathers of these two young stars. Gary Yates, whose father was a stalwart opening bat at Denton St Lawrence CC, went on to have a long career at Lancashire CCC.

Of the overseas contingent, it was the Sri Lankans that stood out. That country was on the verge of Test status, but the names were not yet 'big' enough to gain the players employment in the lucrative major leagues.

Roy Dias played for Denton St Lawrence, Sidath Wettimuny for Denton West, and Duleep Mendis for Poynton. When Sri Lanka met England at Lord's in 1984 Wettimuny made 190, so we could feel a bit better about what he had done to us.

Mendis captained his country in that Test and made 111 and 94. My memory insists that Prestwich fast bowler Cliff Trainor got him out second ball!

One of the charms of the League was the overall quality of the umpiring. Like the players, some were better than others, but all were fair-minded; none was biased.

One gentleman in particular was adored by the players – most of us, anyway. Jack Price was known as a character. He was, first and foremost, a good umpire, and we respected him for his accurate decision-making. The game was rarely dull when Jack was around.

I remember sitting on a bar-stool at Prestwich, late into the night, as Jack spent his match fee while entertaining us with his stories. He had umpired at Bollington CC recently, where he had crossed swords with the autocratic captain of that club, a headmaster not used to being contradicted or trifled with.

The River Bollin runs just outside the boundary of this pretty Cheshire ground and, Jack told us, in the first over of the match a short ball had been hooked into the river and lost. Jack produced the spare ball, in accordance with league rules.

The captain was having none of it. "I know it's a league

Chesterfield 2013

Chesterfield 2013

Glossop CC 2004

Belper Meadows CC 2011

Stone CC 2004

Prestwich CC 2015

Newton Heath CC 2003

Chester-le-Street 2015

Colwyn Bay CC 2013

Canterbury 2008

Tunbridge Wells 2007

Grace Road, Leicester, 2012

Hove 2011

Arundel 2014

Chelmsford 2010

Lord's Cricket Ground 2014

regulation, Jack, but the Laws of Cricket say that a lost ball should be replaced by one of similar wear. And that was brand new. I'll get a new one from the clubhouse."

Jack allowed him to do it, but then asked to see the ball, which was handed to him. Suddenly he started running towards the river. "Similar wear," he said, "but the other one was in the river, wasn't it? So fish this out and bowl with it!" Splash!

"Who does he think I am?" Jack asked us at Prestwich. "One of his schoolkids?"

I had loved my time at Prestwich, but in the 1980s things started to turn a bit sour for me. There was no problem, no falling out, except for a major team bust-up following a Lancashire Cup trip to Lancaster, where we had been humiliated by their pro, Mike Staziker. However, I felt in a rut, and in 1982 I joined Newton Heath CC, who were then newcomers in the same league.

For a few seasons I oscillated between the two clubs until, in 1987, I moved for the last time. I played for Newton Heath until I was well past it. Then I continued to play for a few seasons more.

Like many a club cricketer, I know I was a better player at forty-five than I had been at twenty-five. My time at Newton Heath was perhaps even more fun than my years at Prestwich had been.

We had a good team at Newton Heath in the 1980s, but facilities were basic, with plenty of heavy locks and chains and barbed wire, as we fought a losing battle in a rough area. Our sight-screens and covers were routinely vandalised, though the pitch and outfield were good, far better than at Prestwich, to be honest…while we still had the equipment to maintain them.

During every match we had to bring in the stumps at the tea interval, because otherwise the local kids would jump over the wall and nick them. Eventually the problems wore the club down, we fell into lesser leagues and good players left.

For my photograph, I have selected an incident from 2003, when the club was in the now defunct Manchester Association. What is going on here is a 'bowl out'. Two attempts to play a Cup match had been washed out, so now the two teams are each aiming twelve balls at undefended stumps, as the rain continues to fall.

Newton Heath won 2–0, but in the ensuing years the club has struggled to survive. A new Greater Manchester Cricket League, due to start in 2016, is perhaps the last hope, and at the time of writing Newton Heath has become the fifty-second club to join what appears to be an exciting venture.

Fingers crossed. I believe it really matters for the soul of our game that cricket should be played in the inner city, as well as in the leafy suburbs and the rural shires.

4

DURHAM – IT'S GRAND UP NORTH

The previous chapter concludes what I might term the autobiographical part of my book. I've finished with work, and I can't play any more, so I'm free to wander the shires to watch the game I love.

On many of the trips I am accompanied by Dave Murphy, a long-time friend from our Newton Heath playing days. He's a Lancashire man, but sound in judgement for all that. Usually.

One place we have not yet enjoyed together is Chester-le-Street, the beautiful home of Durham CCC, but it's a rare trip where I don't meet someone I know, even if I travel alone. The Yorkshire away support is large and loyal, during the bad years no less than the recent seasons of plenty.

I have seen some tremendous cricket on this jewel of a ground. The home side has been very strong for many years now, and I recall a match in 2004 when Shoaib Akhtar opened the bowling against Yorkshire. There can have been fewer faster spells in county championship history.

But the day belonged to Anthony McGrath, who paved the way for an eventual Yorkshire victory with a superb 126. A great player of fast bowling, our Mags, who seemed particularly to relish his trips to County Durham.

More recently, 2015 featured a partnership of 366 for the seventh wicket, unbroken, between Jonny Bairstow and Tim Bresnan. Another White Rose victory.

The photograph was taken in 2015.

Yorkshire have lost games, as well as won them, at Chester-le-Street. It's just that I can't quite remember those…

Durham CCC has been one of the success stories of county cricket. I have relished Paul Collingwood and Steve

Harmison, and Nick Speak captained them for a while, a lad I knew well from Manchester. Of the current team, Mark Stoneman makes hundreds against Yorkshire for fun, a seriously good player. There's a guy called Stokes, too.

On one of my trips I met an old man, even older than me, who had been a Yorkshire member before Durham achieved First Class status. We spoke of many things, and he must have been very knowledgeable about cricket because we nearly always agreed!

Ben Stokes I wasn't sure about at the time. I'd seen him as a coltish teenage bowler, and he had never made any runs when I was there. How good was he?

The next Botham, the next Flintoff, was my new friend's assessment. I think he may have been right.

There are cricket enthusiasts like him everywhere, so come with me on a tour of the country. I'm mostly watching Yorkshire, but not exclusively so, enjoying good cricketers (and some not so good) on grounds of all types, from Colwyn Bay to Lord's, before our journey ends at the Best Place in the World.

5

NOWHERE NEAR GLAMORGAN

I once walked through Sophia Gardens to get to the Millennium Stadium, where England were about to lose at rugby – a horrible, wet day in what should have been the spring of 1989 – but I have never seen cricket in Cardiff.

I know Colwyn Bay is not in Glamorgan, but that is where I have watched them play, many times, and it is where my photo was taken in early May 2013; Lancashire were the opponents.

It is one of my very favourite venues, even though I was once cold-shouldered by a couple of locals who started speaking Welsh the moment I sat next to them. I had travelled alone that day.

My very first visit was in 2000 when, on a whim, I went there because Steve James was close to a triple century overnight. I was rewarded not only by seeing him achieve that, but also by a spectacular cameo innings from Matthew Maynard.

It was the first time I had seen a total of 700 on a scoreboard; 718 for three, it finished. Sussex (with a youngster called Mike Yardy making his debut) were the outplayed visitors, beaten by an innings. Big Yorkshire lad Alex Wharf took five wickets in the first innings, and he got Yardy out twice in the game.

In terms of playing area, Colwyn Bay must be the smallest ground on the county circuit. I do have a problem with large grounds made artificially small by boundary ropes – it really annoys me! – but if this is the way the place was built, no problem; variety is the very spice of cricket.

It is a wonderful place to watch cricket on a summer's day, the grassy bank at the far end, from where my photo was taken, being the favoured spot. You may need to move quickly if someone like Maynard is batting.

Apart from the James innings, my strongest memory of Colwyn Bay comes from 2003. Yorkshire had signed the Indian batsman Yuvraj Singh for part of that summer. By all accounts he had settled in well and was popular with his new teammates, but the poor lad couldn't make a run.

We were standing near the exit gate when Yuvraj walked out to bat, and my friend Dave Murphy remarked to me, "He looks like a man walking to the gallows."

We had both been to that dark place, every cricketer has, but it must be doubly dark when it is your profession and you're miles away from home in a foreign land.

6

MEDIUM-FAST DOWN IN KENT

When you come from a place where people greet you with "ey up" and are prone to start sentences "nah, si thee" it can seem an awfully long way down to the bottom right-hand corner of the country, both physically and culturally.

I went to New Zealand once, and that wasn't as far as Kent. You know, I really would like to like Kent. There's all that history! In the cricket museum I saw a ball that had been bowled by Alfred Mynn. Alfred Mynn!

With his tall and stately presence, with his nobly moulded form,
His broad hand was ever open, his brave heart was ever warm;
All were proud of him, all loved him. As the changing seasons pass,
As our champion lies a-sleeping underneath the Kentish grass,
Proudly, sadly will we name him – to forget him were a sin.
Lightly lie the turf upon thee, kind and manly Alfred Mynn.

If ever I get abandoned on a desert island, I'll have the Penguin Cricketer's Companion with me, please, and you can chuck the music into the ocean.

The verse, which is in that best of all cricket books, is attributed to William Jeffrey Prowse.

I have also read about Colin Blythe and Tich Freeman and Frank Woolley. I saw Colin Cowdrey bat and Derek Underwood bowl, and Alan Knott was the best wicketkeeper ever. Rob Key is a modern player I particularly admire.

Unfortunately, my trips down to Canterbury have been mostly miserable. Accommodation had always been rubbish, and expensive, until I discovered an excellent and friendly pub on Wincheap, the King's Head.

The cricket is usually played on a slow pudding of a pitch. That's when it doesn't rain. And inside the ground I often find myself sitting next to, or near, a complete idiot.

You have a choice, as a visiting supporter. You can sit with your own kind, which, with Yorkshire, means listening to incessant grumbling about the price of parking, the price of beer, the cost of everything.

It's all justified in Kent, but I prefer to move about a bit. One time, when I was sitting in the Les Ames Stand, a guy quite a few yards away – but he had a voice like WD-40 – was lecturing his mate about bowling speeds.

He had his Playfair out and was explaining the difference between a fast-medium bowler and one who was rated medium-fast.

"Here, for example, we have Amjad Khan, who is fast-medium, and Tim Bresnan, who is medium-fast. Now that doesn't mean that Bresnan can't bowl a fast-medium ball, if he wants to, nor that all of Khan's deliveries are necessarily fast-medium..."

He went on, and on, and on. When he started to use his Playfair to compare the heights of the players, I knew it was time to move while sanity was still mine.

My photo of Canterbury was taken in July 2008. It is, of course, a lovely place on a fine summer's day.

For my one and only trip to Tunbridge Wells, in June 2007, I drove down the night before. There has to be a worst and most unfriendly hotel in the world, somewhere, and to be fair this one was not in Kent, but just over the border into East Sussex.

"You will really enjoy Tunbridge Wells at this time of year, with the rhododendrons in full bloom," I had been told back home. Well, I didn't. After a night in that place I wasn't in the mood to enjoy anything.

The blooms were fine, if not exceptional. There were rhododendrons in Wibsey Park when I was a kid. It is not the most attractive plant in the world, and is officially classified as an invasive foreign species. And it's poisonous!

More harmful even than an alien-invader bush was the pitch produced for this match. Puddings like this are killing county cricket. The match was doomed to a bore-draw from the first day.

I was amused at the start of a day's play when the announcer told us that Darren Gough was opening the bowling from the railway end.

"Railway end!" exclaimed a very Tunbridgean voice. "Where does he think we are, bloody Leeds?"

He probably wouldn't know, but there is a line, deep in a narrow cutting, behind the western stand at Headingley, very like the one behind the Tunbridge rhododendrons. Neither is obvious from inside the ground.

Spectator facilities were poor, and I found I had to stand to see the cricket at all. Still, I do want these 'outgrounds' to survive, and I am quite happy to endure some discomfort as long as the cricket is good, for which the pitch has to be better than this one. Perhaps I'll be luckier, and in a more receptive mood, next time.

Our game could certainly do with a strong Kent, as in the old days.

7

ANOTHER FOUR AT LEICESTER

The evocatively named Grace Road, Leicester, has long been one of my very favourite venues. But a county that was once strong – champions as recently as 1998 – seems to have fallen on hard times.

On my last visit there, watching Lancashire in 2015, there was but a handful of home spectators, including two old chaps near the sight-screen, who were entering the details into a scorebook.

Steven Croft was making a big score for Lancashire.

"Another four," sighed the first man, writing it in his book.

"Aye," sighed his mate. "Four more."

This little litany was repeated, many times, with minor variations.

The photo was taken during Yorkshire's visit in July 2012, a game in which Adam Lyth scored a wonderful double century. The sun shone, the hanging baskets were lovely and the view from the little stand above the Fox Bar is one of the best in all of county cricket.

In 2005, at Grace Road, I saw Yorkshire skittled out by Ottis Gibson, who took six for 56 and was about as unplayable as a bowler could be. I watched this from another excellent vantage point, the convenient first-floor breakfast room, square with the wicket.

"Don't worry," said a Leicestershire supporter, "he won't do it again."

Pessimism seems to come naturally to the folk of the East Midlands, but he was proved right. Yorkshire were set over 400 to win, and got them easily, thanks to McGrath's 165 not out. I loved watching him bat, more so than his internationally famed contemporary, Michael Vaughan. A lovely venue, is Grace Road, but it is in a dismal area and one fears for the future of a club that has produced so many fine players, Stuart Broad, James Taylor and Luke Wright among them.

8

GOOD OLD SUSSEX BY THE SEA

This is my favourite southern county, and I was devastated when they got relegated in 2015. I have so many memories of Hove. Of Arundel, too, but mostly of friendly, no-nonsense Hove, and I will miss going down there in 2016.

I've seen Yorkshire get some terrible pastings there, over the years. I've watched Murray Goodwin bat for longer than it takes empires to rise and fall.

In 2007 Sussex made 597 for eight before bowling Yorkshire out for 247 and (following on) 89. Having seen the Yorkshire body language and discerned what was coming, I went for a walk on the Downs, that final day. Good choice!

But I've seen some triumphs, too, and some great cricket from Yorkshire, as well as from the home team.

I've met some very odd people at Hove, including a man who was wearing a hat called Hamlet.

"All my hats have names," he explained, "and this one is called Hamlet." Why he chose to impart this knowledge to a bunch of Yorkshire folk is not clear.

Another guy came up to me and told me my name. "You're Dave Morton," he said.

"I know I am," I replied. A strange encounter. Same day as Hamlet. There must be summat in t' watter, down there.

Once, at Hove, I was bought a pint by the Sussex Chief Exec. This has never happened to me at Headingley, I can reveal, but one lives in hope.

My photo, taken from the Pavilion Stand, is from the Yorkshire game in 2011.

Over at pretty Arundel, I have met some pretty odd people, too. One of them is a Yorkshireman whose name is known to me. He was annoyed that he wasn't allowed to take his car into the ground, when others clearly were.

His friends pointed out that the enormous 4x4 he was glaring at had a disabled sticker on it. He thought about this for a moment.

"Look," he said, "he can't be all that disabled. How could a disabled bloke get a sticker as high as that?"

Still chuckling at this archetypal Yorkshire idiot, Dave Murphy and I went over to the little food kiosk, where we encountered the southern equivalent. This man was immaculately turned out, from his striped tie to his polished brown brogues, and he wanted a smoked salmon sandwich.

"Sorry, sir, we haven't got any," apologised the young girl.

"No, no, no," he replied. "Look! It says here 'smoked salmon sandwiches', and I want one!"

"Well, sorry, sir, but we have run out."

"Then you're totally incompetent," he fumed.

I wish the pitch at Arundel matched the surroundings, but good pitches at the outgrounds are the exception – Chesterfield and Scarborough – rather than the rule.

It was tough to choose a picture to represent Arundel, which looks superb from every angle, but in the end I went for one from June 2014. This was a game that was ruined by the pitch, though it did contain one poignant moment when young Jack Leaning, on the very brink of a maiden first-class century, was deceived and dismissed by James Tredwell, bizarrely on loan to first-division Sussex from second-division Kent.

We all knew Jack would score hundreds in the future – which he duly did – but your heart would have to have been made of stone not to feel for him at that moment.

9

NO-NONSENSE ESSEX

Just one game, and only two days of it. That's my experience of Essex. A game that, in July 2010, featured centuries by Alastair Cook and Ravi Bopara – two of them in Ravi's case – and an opening spell by Tino Best that was, absolutely, the Tino Worst.

It was a shame because I loved Tino, a photographer's dream if any cricketer ever has been. He was a real trier, too, but after this it was clear his days with Yorkshire were numbered.

I enjoyed the Chelmsford ground. Small and friendly, it reminded me a bit of Scarborough's cockpit atmosphere. Attendance was good, as the picture shows, and the natives were friendly, even though the Yorkshire mob had got there early and pinched their favourite seats behind the bowler's arm.

First impressions are so important. Fumbling to find my YCCC membership card, I was holding up the queue. The man on the gate smiled and waved me through anyway. Suppose I had been an impostor, sitting in a member's seat? The fabric of the universe might have been torn, irrevocably.

I was in Chelmsford only for a couple of days, because I had chosen to go to Headingley to watch the historic Test between Pakistan and Australia. Attendance was about the same as in Essex, the stewarding a good deal less friendly, a consequence of international sport and the times we live in, I know.

It doesn't mean I have to like it. Very soon I was regretting not having stayed down in cheerful Chelmsford.

10

MIDDLESEX AT LORD'S

I think northerners fall into two categories: those who love London and all the unique attractions it offers, and those who find it impersonal, intimidating and mostly horrible.

I come into the second category, but I have to accept that Lord's is magnificent, even while being irritated by dress codes and the like.

A Lord's Test Match is a wonderful occasion, but this book is not about that. The apparent indifference of Londoners to county cricket makes it an empty, echoing place for a championship match, so I'll submit my photograph and move on.

Contrary to some views, I have always found the people at Lord's (gatemen, stewards, etc) to be excellent and friendly, and ground admission is cheaper than at most places.

The photo was taken in April 2014, a game that Yorkshire had dominated for two and a half days, but which was won for Middlesex by a fantastic Chris Rogers double century.

My only previous visit, for a county game, had been one year earlier, when Yorkshire had played superbly throughout.

I had missed the first day, when Alex Lees made his maiden century, but I saw Andrew Gale reach three figures the next morning. Yorkshire then caught everything, absolutely everything, to take twenty wickets for an eventual ten-wicket win. It was a significant game for a newly promoted team, proof that they could be a force at the higher level, as they were to show.

In 2015 Yorkshire actually won the title at Lord's. Mathematically won it. I didn't bother driving down because it would have taken an asteroid strike to prevent the championship being won there and, as I have indicated, London is not my favourite place.

11

NOTTINGHAMSHIRE – WONDERFUL TRENT BRIDGE

Of all the English Test grounds, Trent Bridge is my favourite, and it is the one that best embraces county cricket, too. Invariably, Notts have a good team. The architecture is beautiful, old and new in harmony; spectators are wonderfully catered for, and treated as valued guests; and the view from the Radcliffe Road Stand is second to none.

No Yorkshireman who was there will ever forget the championship-winning game in 2014, but I have other fond memories, too. Memories of a very young and tearful Joe Root just missing out on his maiden First Class century but, in the same game, Jonny Bairstow getting his, and going on to double it up. 2011, that was.

You will not be surprised that I chose the 2014 game for my photograph. It was September, of course, end of season. Four days for Yorkshiremen to cherish for ever.

The game owed it to us, I think. We had won just one championship title in forty-six years, and that was 2001. I feel our success was well received. Supporters of other counties liked the type of cricket we were playing, and approved too that we had done it with so many home-grown youngsters.

At Trent Bridge we stuck to the successful formula: bat once, bat long. Adam Lyth delighted with his cover driving; the rest just ground it out against demoralised bowlers.

It was expected that Adil Rashid would be key with the ball. In the event he scarcely got to the crease, as Ryan Sidebottom and Jack Brooks did the business.

The one sadness was that a cruel and vindictive ECB ruling prevented captain Andrew Gale from lifting the trophy.

I wrote at the time, "That was so much fun, I think we should do it again next year." And we did.

Trent Bridge 2014

Old Trafford 2014

Liverpool CC, Aigburth, 2013

Southport & Birkdale CC 2011

Northop Hall CC 2014

Wantage Road, Northampton, 2015

New Road, Worcester, 2015

The Australians take the Field, 2013

May's Bounty, Basingstoke, 2009

Southampton 2011

Bristol 2012

Cheltenham College 2005

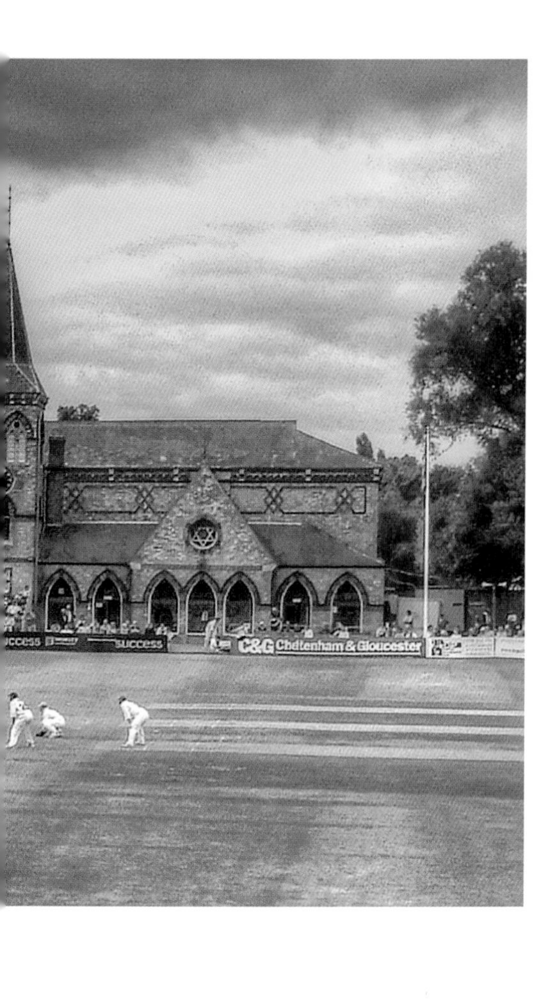
SUCCESS
C&G Cheltenham & Gloucester

Taunton 2014

Edgbaston 2015

Deane & Derby CC, Bolton, 2006

12

MY ADOPTED LANCASHIRE

Old Trafford is only a (free to Seniors) tram ride away from my home and, though I much prefer to watch Yorkshire, I see plenty of Lancashire, too. Occasionally the two clubs even contrive to be in the same division and to play one another.

For my Old Trafford photo I have, not surprisingly, chosen one from August 2014: Yorkshire's championship year. The ground had undergone a major improvement and there was a decent gathering for the Roses Match, by modern standards.

The game went entirely Yorkshire's way, with a double century from Adam Lyth and a century and five-for from Adil Rashid. Payback time, actually, for 2011, and Lancashire ended up the season relegated, a reversal of the events of three years earlier.

The game also featured an amazing slip catch by Kane Williamson, of Steven Croft off Rashid's bowling, possibly the best catch I have ever seen. This book is about scenic shots of grounds, but this was so special I've included the one action shot here.

There is a story behind the photograph itself. I was sitting with a bunch of Lanky mates, and we were square with the wicket, and miles away from the action. They were sitting there because they had always sat there; if the club saw fit to turn the pitch round, that wasn't their problem.

I just happened to be trying to frame a photograph from this hopeless angle and distance, with an uninteresting background too, when the catch occurred. I wasn't even trying for an action shot, but somehow I got the timing right. A complete fluke in every way!

I will add that my Lancashire friends could not have

Kane Williamson catch, 2014

been more complimentary about the Yorkshire team. No bitterness whatsoever, just appreciation of fine cricket. Supporters of the four-day county game are the salt of the earth, wherever you go.

Back in May 2011, in Liverpool – Lancs played most of their games at Aigburth that year because of the rotation of the O.T. square – Lancashire won a thrilling game against Yorkshire.

To make matters even worse, they also won a nailbiter at Headingley, one of the all-time great Roses games, even if the wrong team won.

Lancashire are said to enjoy playing at Liverpool largely because visiting teams do not. Facilities are pretty basic, that is for sure, but there is more atmosphere there than at HQ, as is usually the case with outgrounds.

Lancashire's bowlers seem happier with the surface

there, too, and their supporters believe that playing at Aigburth was a major factor, perhaps the major factor in winning the 2011 title.

My photo comes from a 2nd XI Roses game in 2013, a nice view of the splendid old pavilion.

Lancashire also play at Southport, or Southport & Birkdale CC to give it its full title. If Aigburth is big in playing area, Southport is compact, giving the impression of a big crowd crammed in. As a spectator, you certainly feel involved. I enjoy it. My Southport photo is from July 2011, when Nottinghamshire were the visitors.

I have also watched Lancashire play at Blackpool, many times over the years, but my final photo for this chapter comes from Northop Hall CC, which is actually in Flintshire, North Wales. However, it was the Lancashire home venue for a 2nd XI Roses Challenge match in April 2014.

If the batsman looks familiar, that's because Joe Root was making his comeback to cricket following a hand injury sustained while making a century for England in the West Indies.

Scenic Northop Hall was an excellent venue for a 2nd XI match, a funny moment being provided by three local lads who asked Joe to pose with them for a selfie. They made a mess of taking it and had the nerve to ask him again, to which he agreed, still smiling.

Class act, our Joe, on the field and off. And how wonderful that a small club in the middle of nowhere should be graced for three days by one of the world's best players.

13

PLEASANT NORTHAMPTONSHIRE

My first trip to Wantage Road was in 1966, my last year as a Cambridge student, when I had bought my first car – a black Austin A55 Cambridge (aptly), £75 second-hand.

I remember the ground being pretty gloomy back then, a dual football and cricket set-up, with long grass on the football pitch. There were some good players on show, Mushtaq Mohammad and David Steele, and one against whom I was to play many years later, Brian Crump.

I don't recall seeing Colin Milburn that day, nor David Larter, who at 6'7" was regarded as being freakishly tall. He would have been coming to the end of a brief, but briefly successful, career.

His height led to problems with the then new front-foot no-ball law, and I recall a newspaper headline: 'Larter involved in orgy of no balls.'

From which journalistic low point we move hastily to modern times.

In May 1998, Yorkshire were struggling, having been bowled out by Devon Malcolm's six for 54, but the bowlers were fighting back. The deficit was still not huge when there entered a confident-looking teenager, batting at number eight for the home side.

It was Graeme Swann's 49 that put his team decisively on top, and even more so when he captured three wickets late on day two, including that of Darren Lehmann.

So that was one future England star spotted and predicted, and a second was to follow in 2005.

It was another defeat for Yorkshire, and this time it was the little-known Monty Panesar who did the job, bowling quickly on a turning pitch. Mysteriously, it didn't turn at all when Yorkshire bowled on it, illustrating that Monty was in a different class entirely.

In 2014 occurred an event that had the Yorkshire travelling supporters reaching for their yearbooks. The team had trailed by 115 after being bowled out cheaply first time, but in the second innings Adam Lyth and Alex Lees put on 375 for the first wicket. The old Holmes and Sutcliffe record was never going to be approached, let alone beaten, but this was the fourth highest stand, for any wicket, in the county's history, according to the YCCC Yearbook.

It was good to watch, too. One press report compared the yearbook-waving Yorkies with Mao Tse-tung's followers of yesteryear. I liked that.

The Northampton ground these days is bright and cheerful, with an indoor cricket school where the football pitch used to be: at the Abington Avenue end, which is a good place to sit in the sun.

My photograph was taken on Spring Bank Holiday Monday 2015, when Lancashire were the visitors. Adjacent Abington Park was heaving with thousands of people of all ages, enjoying the wonderful weather.

There were some in the ground, but not enough. They've got their problems at Northampton, which is a shame. It is a lovely place to watch cricket on a summer's day, in a pleasant area, too, and the county club punches well above its weight as a nursery for top players.

14

WORCESTERSHIRE – EVERYONE'S FAVOURITE GROUND

New Road, Worcester, is a lovely ground in a lovely city. The cathedral is, perhaps, not quite as close as the first-time visitor may be expecting – it is across the river, for one thing – but it still looms over the ground.

The decision to chop down some trees has made the view even better, and my photograph from April 2015 shows this.

The ground has changed much, and is due to change more when they demolish the wooden stand on the New Road side. The Graeme Hick Cube is perhaps the least attractive of all the changes, though it is excellent inside – a fine members' facility. I had a ploughman's lunch in there one time, which comprised a decent amount of two cheeses, a very small bread roll and seven golf-ball-sized pickled onions! I was concerned that a hotel development might have ruined the look of the ground but, if anything, it has enhanced it; added a bit of tall building gravitas.

Worcester remains a wonderful and relaxed place to watch county cricket, and I have some fond memories of New Road and the matches I have seen there.

2015 is a good example, when an even game was turned on its head on the third morning by a devastating spell by the Yorkshire bowlers, Steve Patterson five for 11.

I was part of a packed crowd that saw the Australian tourists play there in 2013. Their team included Phillip Hughes, who was later to die so tragically so young; himself a one-time Worcestershire player.

Perhaps the most memorable game of all was played in 2011. Yorkshire were struggling, so much so that they were in danger of following on, until a partnership of 149 between Gerard Brophy (177 not out) and Ryan Sidebottom

Phillip Hughes R.I.P.

turned the game round. Then it was Adil Rashid's turn, and his five for 37 left the team with only a few to win. A very young-looking boy, making his county championship debut, followed a first innings duck with 21 not out.

"I've got a bottle of milk in my fridge that looks older than Joe Root," wrote cricket blogger Dave Hawksworth.

My next memory comes from April 2005. I was sitting in the New Road Stand, almost behind the bowler's arm. With Flintoff batting for Lancashire, I felt I was in a close-catching position there, especially as my right arm was in a sling following a fall the previous week.

Sure enough, a screaming straight drive came my way. The old fellow on my left never even saw it, and I scarcely had time to move before it crashed into the woodwork between us, and just above. Hick had made 176 earlier in the game. He hit the ball hard, too.

If you have not watched county cricket at Worcester, then you must. And no visit is complete without a teatime visit to the Ladies' Pavilion, where the cakes are gorgeous, completely non-fattening, and cheap.

Okay, so I lied about the non-fattening bit.

15

MIXED EXPERIENCES IN HAMPSHIRE

I believe Basingstoke has been described as the most boring town in England. I can see what they mean, sort of, but May's Bounty Cricket Ground was a theatre of pure joy for travelling Yorkshire fans in August 2009.

The background was this. Yorkshire were still in Division One, somehow, but it had been fourteen months since their previous championship win. Fourteen!

Despite that, the travelling support was good, and the home club quickly ran out of white plastic seats. As so often with outgrounds, there was a buzz about the place, and lots of kids there, this being the holiday period.

Yorkshire confidence was low. We supporters reckoned that thirteen catches had been dropped by the team since the last one had been taken.

(This may be complete nonsense, but somehow this figure has stuck in my mind. It may have been, specifically, slip catches. Or simply wrong.)

On a blazing hot day, on a slow pitch, the cricket was attritional. I remember I was stung on the eye by a large insect of unknown species, and I was given first aid by Tim Tremlett, whose son, Chris, was playing in the game. For two days thereafter, I was literally a one-eyed Yorkshire supporter.

The game was meandering until the second half of the Yorkshire innings, when an exhilarating partnership between the two Asian boys, Adil Rashid and Ajmal Shahzad, took the score to 524, a lead of 274.

The draw was still the favourite result, but late on day four Sean Ervine's careless run out triggered a collapse. Six wickets went for 22 runs, and Adil had five for 41 to go with his ton. (Thus inspired, Yorkshire went on to survive the dreaded drop, thanks to a fantastic game at Hove, where David Wainwright was the all-rounder hero. Matthew Hoggard took a hat-trick also, as Sussex were bowled out for 83, losing their last seven wickets for 19.)

Southampton also holds a fond memory for me. The game, in July 2012, featured quite simply the best innings I have ever seen. The weather was awful, all that season, but relented enough for 26 overs to be possible on day one, in which time Yorkshire made 83 for three, with Root 46 not out.

You rarely see, in First Class cricket, a ground where the pitch is the same colour as the square. This one was. Before play started, while other players were having the usual throw-downs, Joe Root had a guy kneeling in front of him and firing balls underarm at his chest, simulating sharp lift from a length. Joe was practising dropping his hands and taking the ball on his body.

On day two, Yorkshire slumped to 108 for six, but Root now took charge. Supported by Azeem Rafiq and Steve Patterson, Joe played like you would dream of playing, ending with 222 not out.

"He will play for England," I perceptively told everyone I met for weeks afterward. No kidding, Sherlock.

It rained throughout the final two days, so that was a long way to go for just 106 overs. We negotiated a refund on our match tickets, we Yorkshire mob, but they wouldn't budge on the car parking fee, that service being 'outsourced', apparently. You could take an instant dislike to anyone who used a word like that.

Joe Root duly made his debut for England in India that following winter. Early in 2013 he scored 182 for Yorkshire at Chester-le-Street. Some, who were present at both games, said it was a better innings that the one at the Ageas Bowl.

All I can say is that it must have been very special indeed!

I don't really warm to Southampton, the Rose Bowl, Ageas Bowl, whatever. Location is poor and attendance must suffer as a result. Against that, there is excellent ice cream, and the members' area is a wonderful facility, perhaps the best anywhere.

My photo is from 2011, in that members' area. I had just paid (*HOW* much?) for a cupcake and coffee.

The ground has been further developed since my last visit. I'd rather go to friendly, boring Basingstoke though, any day.

16

A FROZEN CHICKEN IN GLOUCESTERSHIRE

My last visit to Gloucestershire was in the year it rained for ever; and nowhere did it rain more than at Bristol. Except Canterbury. And Colwyn Bay. Yes, it was damp everywhere in 2012.

A lad called Kane Williamson scored 111 for the 'Shire', but his fine innings was rendered largely irrelevant by the deluge that followed. It took some silly cricket to set up an interesting final day, when Yorkshire chased an 'agreed' target of 400.

Phil Jaques and Gary Ballance made centuries and Yorkshire got the runs easily, a big step towards promotion and the glory years that were to follow.

My photograph comes from this match. I love the grey stone that is a feature at Bristol, a civilised place to watch championship cricket. I understand the ground has been redeveloped substantially since that time.

My previous visit had been on a blazing hot Sunday in 1999, when the same two clubs met in a semi-final of the NatWest Cup, 50 overs.

The day began badly for me, only fifteen miles from home and ridiculously early in the morning, when I tripped a speed camera in South Manchester.

Things improved little down in Bristol as Kim Barnett made 98. The one-day crowd was absolutely mental:

"We can't bat, we can't bowl, but it don't matter, 'cause we're from Gloucester, and we can drive a tractor."

Gloucester was Glaaaaaster, and drive was droive, of course.

They were waving a frozen chicken, for some unfathomable West Country reason. Bonkers, but good fun as the amber nectar flowed. I myself enjoyed a couple of pints from the bar in the Jessop Stand. Now there's a name to conjure with! If I could have just one trip in a time machine I think I'd go back to the Oval, August 1902, when Gilbert Jessop scored 104 in seventy-seven minutes to turn an Ashes Test that was surely lost, with Yorkshire pair Hirst and Rhodes calmly scoring the final 15 runs for a one-wicket win.

Meanwhile, back in 1999, we had the Jack Russell show, the great little man standing up to the stumps as the home medium-pacers strangled the life out of Yorkshire's batsmen.

A super little cameo innings by Gary Fellows gave Yorkshire supporters hope. I must have shown my enthusiasm, because a snotty little twelve-year-old with a public-school accent turned to me and said, "You need ten an over and you're not going to get them."

I hope the lad reached adulthood with all his front teeth intact, but he was right. We fell six runs short of Gloucestershire's 240.

The year before that, I had travelled to Gloucester itself, Archdeacon Meadow, to watch a championship game that the home team had won also, despite eight wickets for Craig White. There was a man called Courtney Walsh…

There were no digital cameras back then, or at least I didn't have one, but I was suitably equipped for my visit to Cheltenham in 2005.

The cricket festival there was an event I had long wished to see, and the College ground lived up to its reputation; gorgeous viewing, from every angle.

I was a bit disgruntled to be charged over the odds to park in a field some distance away but, once inside, the stewards allowed me membership privileges with a YCCC card, even though Gloucestershire were playing Sussex.

One-time Yorkshire hero Steve Kirby was in the home team, but he broke down after only four overs, and Chris Adams' men were far too strong for them.

Choosing which photo to use to represent Cheltenham was a most difficult decision. I hope to return one day. A lovely event.

17

WATCHING MARCUS AT SOMERSET

It is not often, at any sports ground, that you can sit in a stand named after a famous player and watch that same player in action. You can at Taunton though, and I have, many times.

The Trescothick Stand gives you a good, third-man view, from high up and close. It is also handy for the brilliant ice-cream stall. For a behind-the-arm view you want the Botham Stand, which is adorned by a picture of the great man 'failing to get his leg over', in Jonathan Agnew's memorable phrase.

Then there's the Colin Atkinson Pavilion, an outstanding members' facility. This occupies the centre of the photograph I took in 2014, the first game of that season.

There is also a ground-level area, from long-off round towards extra-cover, if the Trescothick Stand is at third-man; a blissful spot in the sun and the preferred location of 'Tractor', a supporter who has become a Somerset legend; a nice man, and very funny. For cricket viewing, Taunton is second to few.

The Worst Day in the History of the World happened while I was in Taunton. The year was 2011 and I had travelled down there with Dave Murphy to watch Lancashire try to win the County Championship for the first time since 1934.

Yorkshire were at Worcester, but there was no point in going there because the White Rose was doomed. All that remained was to see whether Lancashire could win.

I bought a Somerset cap to show which side I was on, though I was pleased, to be honest, when Lancashire pulled the victory off. It was a good game, too, in which James Hildreth and Peter Trego made centuries for the home team, but Lancashire toiled heroically and were rewarded with an eight-wicket win. I am told that in the book that commemorates Lancashire's title I am in the photograph of the trophy presentation. I was particularly pleased for the Lancashire captain, Glen Chapple; if any cricketer ever deserved his day in the sun, it was Chapple. Well done, Lancashire! Once every seventy-seven years, just like Halley's Comet!

Yorkshire wins at Taunton have been hard to come by, these last few seasons, but I was present in 2003 when a wonderful bowling performance by Steve Kirby and a Matthew Wood double century led to a victory by ten wickets.

Yorkshire's last win at Taunton in the championship came in 2008. Racked by pessimism, I missed the final act, driving my car round the Somerset lanes as Yorkshire sneaked home by just 40 runs.

More recently, pitches at Taunton have been very flat, and the Somerset tactic has been to con ('persuade' or 'encourage' might be kinder) Yorkshire into a declaration. To my horror, Yorkshire fell for this tactic not once, but twice, in 2009 and 2010. Somerset won without Yorkshire help in 2011.

So my memories of Taunton are of batsmen scoring runs. Trescothick, naturally, Hildreth, Suppiah and Trego. The Yorkshire lads, too, but the Somerset runs were winning runs.

It follows, therefore, that I admire the poor blokes who earn their living by having to bowl on this thing, and I mention Andy Caddick and Charl Willoughby as two who toiled endlessly and skilfully in the Somerset cause.

It would be pleasant, one season soon, to drive down to that beautiful county and to find a pitch more conducive to a good, even game of cricket.

Cricket is best when bowlers are marginally on top.

18

SPLENDID WARWICKSHIRE

Edgbaston has undergone a major development these last few seasons. One Warwickshire member told me that they didn't need a big wrecking ball to demolish the old pavilion; just a push was enough.

The new one is enormous, set up for Test cricket rather than the county championship, and I always sit on the other side, in the RES Wyatt Stand, where it is warmer, and where the locals are friendly and knowledgeable.

I do not need a long memory to find a happy one of Edgbaston. In 2015 Yorkshire bravely batted first on what looked a very green pitch, and were bowled out for 213. Jonny Bairstow, playing perhaps the finest innings of his life, scored more than half of these.

It was predictable that the home side, too, would find batting difficult. So difficult, in fact, that they only just saved the follow-on with their last pair at the wicket. Ryan Sidebottom had six for 34.

Vying with the Yorkshire pair for man of the match were the Edgbaston ground staff. With bands of heavy rain moving across, play would be halted, the ground staff would work feverishly for an hour or more, and play would restart just in time for the next downpour.

This sequence was repeated half a dozen times. For them to work so hard when it was Yorkshire on top in the game is a tribute to their professionalism.

I will mention just one more Yorkshire visit, another victory. I can't remember us losing there, to be honest, but in 2010 it seemed we were going to.

Warwickshire had set Yorkshire 291 to win, a target that seemed distant indeed when captain Gale was out at 123 for five. Leg-spinner Imran Tahir appeared to have Yorkshire completely in his pocket.

Twenty-year-old Jonny Bairstow changed the game with a brilliant 81, while Jacques Rudolph added solidity at the other end; classical cricketing nous. The task had seemed impossible, but Yorkshire won by four wickets, with Jonny B out just before the end.

One of Birmingham's best-kept secrets is Cannon Hill Park, just across the road from the cricket ground. It is a delightful spot, a great place to eat your lunch and watch the ducks on the pond. For a county game you can park your car there, too, and for free.

Well done Warwickshire, in every way, and any county that can provide an Ian Bell for my pleasure will always get my vote.

19

SORRY, SURREY

Our journey round the shires is almost complete. Just one remains, the Greatest County of All.

However, I do owe my readers an apology, because one almost-as-great cricketing county is entirely absent from the photograph pages. There is no Kennington Oval, no Surrey, not even a club ground.

It could be thought a dark conspiracy on my part, revenge for a Yorkshire childhood made miserable by Stuart Surridge, May and Bedser, Lock and Laker. We had great players in the 1950s; Surrey had a great team.

I hated them for it, back then. Nowadays I don't hate anyone except, perhaps, those who would destroy or diminish county cricket.

Ironically, as I grew up, I found Surrey players to be among my favourites: Ken Barrington above all, and even the aforementioned Tony Lock. How could anyone not admire grand battlers like these?

Later came Mark Butcher and Graham Thorpe.

However, to date, I have never watched a county game in Surrey, so I have no photograph to show. I have attended the Oval several times to watch Test cricket, though Dean Jones scored a century the most recent time, which was 1989.

My strongest memories are from 1963. Wes Hall's glorious run-up will remain with me for ever. More modern readers can picture the sprinting Shoaib Akhtar, but Hall's pure action was the more pleasing to the eye. Facing him was Brian Bolus, a Yorkshire blocker who had reinvented himself as a Notts dasher, and he hit Hall back over his head, amazingly, spectacularly, off the back foot, new ball and all!

Wormsley (with red kite) 2005

Todmorden CC 2015

Flixton CC, near Filey, 2013

Brooksbottom CC, Bury, 2004

Sheffield Collegiate CC 2008

Stamford Bridge CC, near York, 2011

The Wall at York CC, 2014

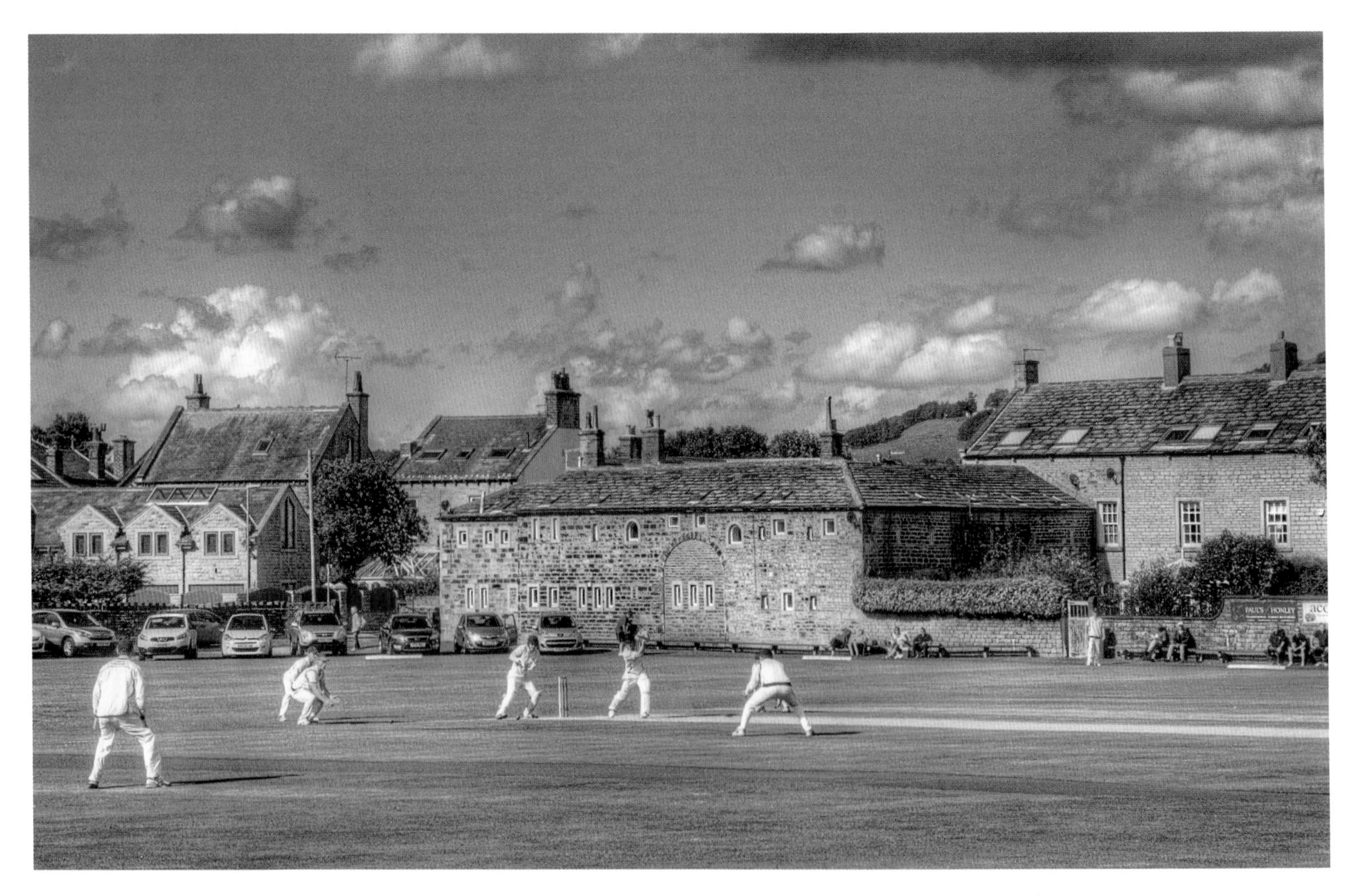

Honley CC, Huddersfield, 2015

Headingley 2015

Scarborough CC 2009

Lunch Interval 2013

In the same game I remember the great Brian Close keeping wicket, deputising for an injured Jim Parks, and a match-winning innings of breathtaking brilliance from Rohan Kanhai.

I also remember beer being two shillings and sixpence a pint, which was so outrageous I didn't buy any. You can take the boy out of Yorkshire…

On another visit in 1985, I witnessed the final demolition of a demoralised Aussie team, as England made 376 for three on the first day, with centuries for Gooch and Gower.

I am due to watch a county game at the Oval in 2016; my hotel room is booked. My photographs will appear on Flickr in due course, but cannot be in this book.

Instead, I am going to present a few images from around the country, a miscellany of grounds that found no place in earlier chapters.

The first two could not be more different: Deane & Derby CC in Bolton, Lancashire, complete with dark satanic mill; and Wormsley in Buckinghamshire, where the red kites fly, the private ground of the late Sir Paul Getty.

I played at Deane & Derby many times in the long twilight of my career. It could be interesting, and pleasant on a nice day. They were (and are, I imagine) an all-Asian club. Teas there could be spicy, but not half as tasty as some of the players who turned out for them.

I remember fielding at slip for two long hours while one particular batsman made light of our bowling. The following week we turned up at Winton CC, and there he was again, acting as their pro!

He denied he was the same man, and the name in the scorebook was different, but he looked the same, and he came out with the same bat, which had 'Ahmed' written in large ballpoint letters on the back.

I should know; I had been staring at it long enough last Saturday.

That game was the last time I made a significant score for Newton Heath 1st XI, 47 good runs, before I hit the longest of long-hops from off-spinner 'Ahmed' straight to mid-wicket. I was fifty years old – or maybe fifty-one – and the chance never came again.

No regrets. My photo of Deane & Derby comes from

2006, a day on which one of my successors as opening bat, a mere slip of a lad (comparatively), made a century. Well played, 'Ozzy' Osborne!

I liked him. When he had batted well he would announce, in a Caribbean accent, "I was seeing the ball like a breadfruit, man."

The Wormsley photograph comes from May 2005, when Buckinghamshire were playing Lancashire in the Cheltenham & Gloucester Trophy. Dave Murphy and I had driven down through awful weather, and we were rewarded for our optimism with some cricket.

My chief memory, apart from the stunning setting, was of the red kites circling the ground. I spent ages trying to get a good photograph of both bird and cricket. In the end I faked it, a spot of copy and paste. Not a lie, just a different sort of truth.

My next stop takes us to the Pennines and the Yorkshire/Lancashire border. Todmorden CC is a wonderfully scenic ground, and is used by both counties for 2nd XI and age-group fixtures.

I love going to Tod. In addition to the cricket ground, there's an excellent market, with an outstanding cheese stall, a friendly fish and chip cafe in the marketplace, and the Rochdale Canal with its spectacular 'Great Wall of Tod', which is said to contain four million bricks. The railway runs along the top of it.

The cricket ground is relatively long and narrow, and affords beautiful views from every angle. I particularly like the one with the Stoodley Pike Monument in the background, and the picture I have chosen was taken in July 2015 during a Roses under-17 clash.

My next choice for this chapter could just as well have been placed in the Yorkshire or Scarborough chapters. If you're travelling on the A64 towards Scarborough, you will come to a large roundabout at Staxton, where the main road veers left, towards Seamer. Stay instead on the Filey road, and soon you will see Flixton CC on the right, just after the village.

This lovely little ground, nestling in the foothills of the Yorkshire Wolds, is one of my favourites anywhere.

My final photo in this section comes from Brooksbottom CC, near Bury, Lancashire. The slope is the biggest

I ever played on, side to side, just like Lord's! The pitch isn't much to write home about, if you're a batsman, though three of the boundaries are temptingly close.

Forget all that! It's an absolutely superb setting. My photograph shows action from a Manchester Association 2nd XI Cup Final in September 2004. The home team are impersonating Australians in green and gold, Newton Heath are in blue.

The structure on the hill is the Peel Monument, which towers over nearby Ramsbottom. That's Sir Robert Peel, Prime Minister and the 'father of modern policing', who was born in Bury.

Newton Heath lost the game.

20

BACK TO YORKSHIRE

This is where my journey started, watching my dad play for Great Horton in the Bradford League, games with my mates in Wibsey Park, and then my first set of whites, first cricket bag (with slot for bat), for games afternoons at Bradford Grammar School.

The bat was, of course, a Gradidge Len Hutton Autograph. Anything else would have been unthinkable.

I could watch our Len in action, too, just a bus ride from Wibsey to the Park Avenue ground, where Yorkshire used to play about four games a season. Quickly I got to recognise all the players: Hutton, of course, and Frank Lowson, who resembled a pale shadow of the master; left-handers Vic Wilson and Willie Watson; Norman Yardley the captain; big-hitting Johnny Wardle, the kids' favourite; and the already legendary Fred Trueman.

There were two others, about whom my grammar school friend Malcolm and I would argue endlessly. He favoured Raymond Illingworth, but I was in the Brian Close camp. We knew there was something special, really special, about both these two young players.

I think we were proved correct!

I must also mention Jimmy Binks. When I started watching Yorkshire, the wicketkeeper was Don Brennan, then it was Roy Booth, who moved to Worcestershire. Then came Binks.

Watching modern-day keepers, and remembering the great Binks, makes me scream with frustration. Cricket has moved on, things have improved, largely, but…

Okay. Time to shut up and move on also.

Back then, as a little kid and into my teens, I watched county cricket at Bradford, at Headingley occasionally, and also at Bramall Lane in Sheffield. These were the three major Yorkshire grounds.

I recall also a game at Fartown, Huddersfield, where the rugby league team used to play. There was a clock tower there dedicated to the 'Great Triumvirate' (Rhodes, Hirst, Haigh), which was pointed out to me. Yorkshire history runs deep and proud.

As a family our holidays were always to Scarborough Festival, and I will finish this book with a whole chapter on t' best place in t' world.

Time passed. Family Morton left Yorkshire, but the 1960s brought in a new age, a Golden Age. With Trueman, Binks, Close and Illingworth the elder statesmen now, with Stott, Taylor, Padgett, Hampshire, Boycott, Nicholson, Richard Hutton, Don Wilson, how could a team like this not win?

They won all right, just seven Championships in ten seasons. Then came the famine years, but by now I was working all week and playing every weekend, so I followed and mourned from afar.

By the time I had retired, first from work, later (sadly) from cricket, Yorkshire were slowly building again. I became a member in 1994, took up photography with my first digital camera in 2002, and the rest you know, if you've read the book so far.

Selecting Yorkshire photographs was difficult, from so many. In Sheffield, with Bramall Lane now entirely lost to football, Yorkshire played at Abbeydale Park, which was a glorious drive for me, through Derbyshire from Manchester. An attractive venue, too, which I always enjoyed, and home ground of Sheffield Collegiate CC.

My photograph was taken in June 2008, a Yorkshire 2nd XI match against Scotland.

I also saw a couple of county 1st XI games at Harrogate, before that venue, too, was abandoned. The 2nd XI still plays at several highly attractive grounds, of which Todmorden (previous chapter), York and Stamford Bridge are my favourites.

I love these 2nd XI fixtures: the keen youthfulness of the players, the hardcore cricket-nut supporters, the pride of the host club, all in evidence. If anything represents the hope for years to come, it is these games.

I have a particular fondness for Stamford Bridge CC. It is a gorgeous place to be on a summer's day, when the only sound is the faint drone of a light aircraft in the big sky. The club really puts on a show, and one day I *will* win a tombola prize.

I have enjoyed some excellent cricket on this ground, and some big hitting, too.

Rob Bailey ended his career with Derbyshire, and Stamford Bridge was not big enough for him. For a while I feared for the safety of my car, then realised that – inside the ground – it was in no danger at all.

Another Derbyshire player, Tony Palladino, scored perhaps the fastest century I have ever seen, at Stamford Bridge. Immense straight hitting was the feature of this innings.

Games there are often well attended, despite the place being miles from anywhere, a little piece of English heaven. I took the photograph on a blissful June day in 2011.

York CC is a very different venue, but no less attractive, with an opulent and large pavilion. Running along one end of the ground, behind the bowler's arm, is an attractive brick wall, with benches for spectators, a lovely place to sit on a warm sunny day. I took the photograph during a Yorkshire v Worcestershire 2nd XI game in 2014.

My fourth Yorkshire ground is one I visited for the first time in 2015, the home of Honley CC, who play in the Huddersfield League. Situated in spectacular 'Summer Wine' country, it is a wonderful place. It has a good-sized playing area too, unlike many in that area.

Honley was the chosen venue for a two-day Roses under-19 fixture, a game that Lancashire won; but not even that could detract from the splendour of the surroundings.

One Lancashire supporter said that this was where he wanted to be if another war came: "The enemy will never find it!"

That leaves just two Yorkshire grounds.

There's Scarborough, which is the subject of my final chapter, and there's Headingley. Of course there's Headingley!

I have an early memory of Headingley, a game against Middlesex in the 1950s. I wanted to see Edrich and Compton, and I can remember one of them edging Bob Appleyard for four, down towards a dark and cavernous rugby stand.

And then it rained, a miserable, cold, thin rain, for the rest of the day. So we went home.

On another miserable day, many years later, Yorkshire

were playing Hampshire in front of a mere scattering of spectators. There were perhaps three of them on the western terrace.

The Hampshire batsman Adrian Aymes was given out lbw, a decision with which he clearly disagreed. One of those spectators advised him to get a move on and leave the ground, please, whereupon Aymes made a bee-line towards that area.

The following day the press reported more crowd trouble on the notorious western terrace. Well, they say "three's a crowd", in a different context.

Mostly the Headingley recollections are happy ones, of sunny days, of big crowds and Yorkshire heroes; I was present the day Geoffrey Boycott made his 100th hundred in the 1977 Ashes Test.

Most of my memories are from Roses encounters. In 2005 Lancashire had had marginally the better of the first three days, but we all felt that their captain Mark Chilton had delayed his declaration in order to complete his own century.

In the end, Yorkshire's target was an unlikely 383 in less than a full day's play.

The late declaration seemed not to matter as Chapple and Anderson reduced the White Rose to a miserable 109 for six. Lancashire now met some resistance, but when Matthew Hoggard walked out to bat at number ten, well over two hours remained.

Richard Dawson fought on for a while, but his dismissal was my signal to leave. There are many things I want to do in life before I have to watch Lancashire beat Yorkshire at Headingley.

I drove westward along the M62 over the Pennines, arrived home, couldn't resist checking the score. And there it was: Yorkshire 273 for nine (Hoggard 64* from 138 balls, Deon Kruis 13* from 55 balls) and the match was drawn. It felt like an innings win.

My final Headingley anecdotes involve Australians. In September 2003 Yorkshire signed Damien Martyn on a short contract. He played two championship matches only, being injured in the first, against Somerset.

On his return to action, against Gloucestershire, he produced for our delight an orgy of batsmanship, 238 runs off only 159 balls. I have seen some astonishing innings, but for prolonged brilliance, never anything like this.

Darren Lehmann was the Yorkshire overseas pro for many seasons. Two innings stand out, even above the outstanding that was the Lehmann norm. There was his 252 against Lancashire in July 2001, a championship-winning season for us; and there was his swansong, a truly magnificent innings of 339 against Durham in the final fixture of 2006.

Headingley has been graced by many a good player, and quite a few great ones; Lehmann was a genius.

For my photo of the Yorkshire HQ I have gone for a cloudy day in June 2015, a tough struggle against Middlesex that Yorkshire just won, by four wickets – and it felt a lot closer than that.

Modern Headingley is fine, a comfortable place to watch cricket, with good facilities, and the pitch nowadays is very good for batting and bowling.

But now it's time to get out the bucket and spade, sunglasses (and thermal blanket), and to head seventy miles north-east to the Best Place of All.

21

SCARBOROUGH, MY SCARBOROUGH

I have travelled the world watching cricket, from the magnificent MCG to manic Mumbai, via Barbados and Galle, Cape Town and Wellington. Fantastic venues, all, but none can compare with Scarborough, the best and happiest place in all of creation.

It was natural that a Yorkshire cricketing family would choose Scarborough Festival for their annual week, back when I was a kid. I had never been abroad. I don't think I had ever met anyone who had been abroad, except for fighting in wars.

I remember my headmaster at Burton GS going absolutely ape because none of us thirteen-year-olds had ever heard of the Dardanelles; so that was one guy who had been overseas on duty, I guess.

There were three three-day matches at North Marine Road in those days: Yorkshire v MCC, Gentlemen v Players and TN Pearce's XI v the Tourists; and that meant Australia in 1953, the year Len Hutton's team regained the Ashes.

I remember being disappointed when it was announced that RR Lindwall on the scorecard was to be replaced by JC Hill – the most famous fast bowler in the world rested in favour of a nondescript and very unfamous leg-spinner!

However, I was to witness a world record as Richie Benaud hit eleven sixes on the final day, and I had already seen the great Len (not yet Sir Leonard) make a hundred. I was happy enough.

As I got older I began to understand that these Festival games were not the real thing. I was being short-changed. 'Friendly' cricket is rubbish – rubbish to watch, rubbish to play, rubbish.

Thankfully, these days, Scarborough is used annually for two county championship four-day matches, as well as some List A one-day games. I have seen some of the best and keenest cricket of my lifetime, these last twenty seasons, at Scarborough.

Adding to the atmosphere is the crowd, often in excess of 4,000 for a day of championship action. You don't see that anywhere else, and the steeply banked seats round a small playing area make for an intense viewing experience.

The memories come thick and fast. Chris Silverwood, omitted from the England touring party, taking it out on Kent, whose Dean Headley had been selected; Ian Blackwell, then with Derbyshire, and David Hussey, an Australian playing for Notts, both demonstrating that Scarborough needed to be about twice as big to contain their hitting power.

I remember also Kabir Ali of Worcestershire taking eight wickets on the damply green first morning of a match, but the most memorable bowling performance of all belongs to Adil Rashid.

It was July 2006 and Darren Lehmann was injured. Young Adil had been making big runs for 2nd XI and Academy, and he was the one chosen to fill the Australian's boots. Temporarily.

Legend has it that captain Craig White asked Adil, "Do you bowl at all?" A story too good not to be true.

It turned out the tiny eighteen-year-old did bowl, a little, and he took a wicket in just his second over, to end an annoying last-wicket partnership.

In the second innings, roared on by an enthusiastic crowd, Rashid baffled and bamboozled the Warwickshire batsmen to take six for 67. Yorkshire had won by an innings, and a career had been launched. It was Steve Patterson's debut, as well as Rashid's – a good day indeed for Yorkshire's future.

More recently, it has been the Yorkshire v Durham clash that has turned North Marine Road into the place where champions are made.

Yorkshire had high hopes in 2013. They were newly promoted and flying high, but they left with their title hopes in tatters.

This was a terrific Durham performance. Mark Stoneman set the tone with a century, there were strong all-round contributions from Ben Stokes and Steve Borthwick, and

Yorkshire were clearly second best, which is where they finished in the season's final reckoning.

Two years later, with a title now behind them, Yorkshire again welcomed Durham to North Marine Road.

In another tremendous and memorable game, Yorkshire recovered from a first-day 95 for nine to win by 183 runs. Rashid had another good Scarborough outing, a century and some second-innings wickets, and Australian Glenn Maxwell also scored a hundred, their partnership putting Yorkshire on top.

The killing blow was provided by Liam Plunkett, a former Durham player, but a Yorkshireman, let it not be forgotten.

Scarborough is a place where old friends meet. In an earlier chapter I mentioned Ken Morgan, who was a veteran player when I started out with Prestwich CC. Always a man to make good decisions, Ken was married to a Yorkshire lass, and he and Pat continued to attend Scarborough Festival until both were well into their eighties.

If Scarborough is a place for the old to meet, it is also for the young. Nothing gladdens my heart more than to see hundreds of kids playing soft-ball cricket on the outfield during breaks in play. Watch carefully, and you will see many of them are playing good cricket. Yorkshire cricket.

Perhaps the best Scarborough memory of all belongs to 2001 and the moment when captain David Byas took the catch at backward point that clinched Yorkshire's first championship title since 1968. The Yorkshire tribe had wandered thirty-three years in the wilderness, and we stood and cheered for hours, uncaring as the rain came teeming down.

Scarborough is the heart and soul of Yorkshire cricket.

A NOTE ON THE PHOTOGRAPHY

Many years ago, when I was still a keen and active cricketer, I acquired my first camera, an Olympus OM1. A film camera, of course.

I would often take it to matches I was playing in. As an opening batsman, if I got out in the early overs, it gave me something to do for a couple of hours, photographing my teammates. This was fun, but never really a hobby. Cricket was my hobby, and rugby in winter, and when I finally lost my camera to burglary I did not grieve too much, nor did I replace it.

I had noticed, however' on those occasions when I attempted to photograph a landscape, that where my eye saw a foreground rich in colour, with interesting sky above, my camera seemed to see very little of either. Get the foreground right, and the sky was washed out, featureless; if the sky was right, the rest of the picture was too dark.

I assumed it was because I was rubbish at photography, and stopped doing landscapes. My cricket and rugby shots were okay.

Many years later, having got my first computer, I eventually plucked up courage and bought a digital camera, spending over £600 on a Fujifilm 6900 Zoom in 2002. I was so frightened of it that it stayed in its box for several months!

Looking back, it was incredibly crude, and actually cost more than my first Canon DSLR. I now use an old Canon EOS 40D as my main camera, and whatever takes my fancy as the smaller, more portable option. I tend to be careless, to drop them on concrete or put them into bags with wet and sandy towels, so I get through a few.

Soon I encountered the old familiar problem with landscapes. I became aware that real photographers used filters, carefully positioned, to cut down the light from a bright sky. I felt this was not for me. Too technical, too much fiddling about. Not spontaneous.

Instead, I attempted to photograph land and sky separately, so both were correctly exposed but in a different photograph. I would then attempt to use 'layers' to combine the two, hoping the join would not look too bad. Sometimes it even worked. I built up a bit of a 'library' of skies I could call upon.

It was while browsing through the photos on Flickr that I came across something very different: vibrant landscapes that actually matched the way I saw the world. And three letters, HDR, started to appear in titles and captions.

Welcome to the world of High Dynamic Range. You take three shots (usually three), different exposures, in quick succession. It is called 'auto-bracketing' and even cheap cameras will do it.

The software now takes over the process. I use Photomatix. You move a few sliders until the picture looks right, press the button and you're done. You can make any final adjustments using your normal photo-editing program.

Somehow, Photomatix also deals with movement between the three shots. It is called 'de-ghosting' and it usually works, so much so that even action cricket shots are possible – though I usually reserve HDR for the wider, scenic view.

I have no understanding of the process whatsoever. But then, I don't know how to make paper, or ink, and that's never stopped me writing.

All the scenic photographs in this book that were taken after July 2012 are HDR. I wanted some unity of style within my book, so the earlier ones have been 'tone-mapped from a single image', which produces a very similar result. You'd call it 'faked', I suppose.

I received help with auto-bracketing and HDR from:

- *Practical HDR* by David Nightingale.
- Trey Ratcliff and his website www.stuckincustoms.com

- Various tutorials on YouTube, some better than others.
- A couple of guys on Flickr who sent me encouragement and good advice.

My own photographs are to be found on Flickr and are available free for anyone to download from www.flickr.com/photos/forwarddefensive/sets

Anyone who saw me bat will understand the 'Forward Defensive' username.

Dave

LIST OF PHOTOGRAPHS

The Author batting at Glossop in 1984 11
Chesterfield 2013 17
Chesterfield 2013 18
Glossop CC 2004 19
Belper Meadows CC 2011 20
Stone CC 2004 21
Prestwich CC 2015 22
Newton Heath CC 2003 23
Chester-le-Street 2015 24
Colwyn Bay CC 2013 25
Canterbury 2008 26
Tunbridge Wells 2007 27
Grace Road, Leicester, 2012 28
Hove 2011 29
Arundel 2014 30
Chelmsford 2010 31
Lord's Cricket Ground 2014 32
Trent Bridge 2014 49
Old Trafford 2014 50
Liverpool CC, Aigburth, 2013 51
Southport & Birkdale CC 2011 52
Northop Hall CC 2014 53
Wantage Road, Northampton, 2015 54
New Road, Worcester, 2015 55
The Australians take the Field, 2013 56
May's Bounty, Basingstoke, 2009 57
Southampton 2011 58
Bristol 2012 59
Cheltenham College 2005 60
Taunton 2014 62
Edgbaston 2015 63
Deane & Derby CC, Bolton, 2006 64
Kane Williamson catch, 2014 66
Phillip Hughes R.I.P. 71
Wormsley (with red kite) 2005 81
Todmorden CC 2015 82
Flixton CC, near Filey, 2013 83
Brooksbottom CC, Bury, 2004 84
Sheffield Collegiate CC 2008 85
Stamford Bridge CC, near York, 2011 86
The Wall at York CC, 2014 87
Honley CC, Huddersfield, 2015 88
Headingley 2015 89
Scarborough CC 2009 90
Lunch Interval 2013 91